The Practice of the Presence of God

Also translated by E. M. Blaiklock

The Imitation of Christ by Thomas à Kempis

The Practice of the Presence of God

Based on The Conversations, Letters,
Ways, and Spiritual Principles of
Brother Lawrence, as well as on
the writings of Joseph De Beaufort

translated by
E. M. Blaiklock

THOMAS NELSON PUBLISHERS
Nashville • Camden • New York

Fourth printing

First published in Great Britain in 1981 by Hodder and
Stoughton, London.

First published in the United States in 1982 by Thomas
Nelson, Inc., Publishers, Nashville, Tennessee.

Published in Nashville, Tennessee, by Thomas Nelson, Inc.
and distributed in Canada by Lawson Falle, Ltd.,
Cambridge, Ontario.

Printed in the United States of America.

ISBN 0-8407-5830-0

Contents

Introduction

Old Acquaintance

Something over half a century ago, there was a second-hand bookshop in a side street in Auckland where I sometimes browsed among the dusty shelves. It was there that I first found Brother Lawrence in a tiny dark-green book of extracts with a few words of introduction. I was looking, absurd as that may sound, for small books. The next year, 1924 in fact, was, by an academic accident, to be a comparatively easy one, so I had what the Germans call a 'wanderyear' before reading for Honours in Latin and French. I sought unencumbered travel; impecunious, it had to be. Books had to be little ones.

In the small book I soon realised that I had a treasure. I had been a Christian for two years and knew all the stress and hard thinking which academic life imposes on an honest young man, seeking to integrate faith, life and learning. In my quest John's Gospel already meant much to me, and here, in the little green book which slipped so snugly into my pocket, I met a cook from a Carmelite monastery kitchen who seemed without effort to turn the haunting last words of Christ into the simplicities of common living.

I looked for more of him in London. That February was a month yellow with the city's sooty untamed fog. But it was warm in the dim old bookshops of the Charing Cross Road, and I fossicked without success for a French text of Brother Lawrence, or

7

anything about the man. So, too, in Paris. I was there in April, lodging below Montmartre. The winter lingered, and it was cold along the Quais where the Seine flowed turgidly, 'liquid history' like Old Thames. The stalls of the bookvendors on the parapets held me for chilly hours as I continued my vain search for Frère Laurent. As far as I can discover, it was not until ten years later that a modern French edition appeared. Had I, therefore, succeeded in my search along the brown river, I might have brought home a real relic of a century in whose literature I was reading deeply, a 1693 first edition, no less.

I was aware that this humble man whose simple piety was reaching out appealingly to me, had real historical significance. We know little enough about him, for all the Abbé De Beaufort's wordy diligence, but enough to see that he is a tiny jewel in the glitter of that age, and an uregarded facet of the religious history in which the half century of Louis the Fourteenth is rich. Protestant scholarship may, indeed, have given too little attention to the very real and beneficent religious movements of the time. Perhaps they have thought too much of the suppression of non-Catholic religion, culminating in Louis' stupid revocation of the Edict of Nantes in 1694, and the Huguenot exodus. Benjamin Franklin, as a boy, in the Old South Church of Philadelphia, was still hearing pulpit thunder against 'that accursed man, persecutor of God's people, Louis the Fourteenth . . .'

But here was someone quite apart from 'history'. How little, in all 'golden ages' do we know of the lives of obscure men. That is part of the value of the New Testament itself. Scarcely anywhere else is the proletariat of the first century to be found. So often in large tracts of history there is little pabulum for those who seek not

the princes and prelates with periwigged charioteers riding triumphantly laurelled to lap the fat of the years, but rather the scorned, the rejected, the men hemmed in by the spears . . . (John Masefield)

This was in my mind as I turned over the worn books under the propped lids of the boxes by the Seine. I had moved with avid interest among the writers of that splendid age. Blaise Pascal was near to my Christian faith. Racine had laid fast hold on me. I still number him among the four supreme dramatists (himself, Shakespeare, Aeschylus and Sophocles). I had delighted in Molière, and found La Fontaine enchanting. I had read some sermons of Bossuet, and some of Fénelon's gracious letters.

Still, as I fingered the small book in my pocket, I felt that there might here be a glimpse behind the royal façade of that significant period, a flash of French life under the Sun-King, not visible elsewhere. Perhaps here was one of 'the Remnant' of which the Old Testament is so vividly aware, the Amos, the Elijah who appears and disappears – and in the New Testament the shepherds, Mary, the 'common people', the old faithful of the land. Just plain Brother Lawrence, neither 'Saint' nor 'Blessed', and there were surely many others like him.

One wonders how he came to the Archbishop's notice. Perhaps, at second-hand or third, some knowledge of the monastery cook touched the edge of a pietistic or 'charismatic' movement in the established Church. 'Quietism' was strong in France during the years of Brother Lawrence's activity. His 'practice of the presence of God' was much more simple, real and involved with living that the passivity of the Quietists at large. Lawrence's 'practice' did not crystallise into a theology in spite of the 'Maxims', the writing of which may have been pressed on the simple man, but it could have been a common situation in which an unknown man finds prominence and even popularity by the unsought embrace of a 'movement'.

At any rate, Madame Guyon published her two mystical books in the last decade of Brother Lawrence's life (*A Short and Easy Method of Prayer* in 1685; *Song of Songs* in 1688). Fénelon was active in writing, preaching and controversy about the same time, and he was deeply inflenced by Madame Guyon. Both Bossuet and Fénelon make passing reference to the Brother. And why did the Archbishop's vicar-general become interested in investigating his way of life?

If there are some threads of history to pick up here, it is quite impossible, on surviving evidence, to tie them together. In 1924 I had no thought of trying. I simply found interest in an unusual contemporary of the great writers I was reading and felt too that here was one who, across the centuries, had something to say to me, words which moved and challenged me.

Is it not most likely that Brother Lawrence knew little of the surge of history outside the monastery walls? If ever he found himself free from demanding duty, he tells us, he would prostrate himself and worship God. When he 'entered religion', Louis, free from both mother and Mazarin, was well embarked on his quest for absolutism and 'la gloire' which was to cost France dearly, lead to military disaster, domestic stress, famine and discontent.

The mental agony of Lawrence's early 'religious'

years must also have been a stern preoccupation. His own spiritual life, given to his dominant ideal of living ever in God's presence, must itself have removed him from the stir and flow of historic events. If he heard of Louis' more private doings, the amours which ruined the life of the pathetic La Vallière, and, under the evil Athenais De Montespan, came near to ruining his own, Lawrence would have simply said that human sin had no limits, and that he was surprised, man being fallen man, that it was not more flagrant.

It is to be hoped that he was left in peace – from Madame De Maintenon, la Guyon, De Beaufort and all the rest. The last named does drop a few words which might suggest a deeper late involvement in affairs than might seem his habit, but there are small grounds for speculation. On the whole allow imagination to leave him in his kitchen, with perhaps some alleviation among the pots and pans as the eighties drew near. He was, perhaps, as was once said of a great Roman, 'happy in the opportuneness of his death'. He did not live to see the stormy setting of Louis' sun, and was gone before the Four Horsemen rode too thunderously to the north, and through the land. He was not driven to pronounce judgment, when religious conscience arose at last to confront the aggressions of the monarch. The kitchen, to the edge of old age, was his realm, hot, smoky, unperturbed and unpreoccupied. We can trust it so remained.

The Brother Himself
Whether my little green book survived the vicissitudes of travel, and came back with me from my wanderyear I cannot say. After the odd fashion of

books, at some time over the years, it has vanished from my library. The first French publications of 1693, two years after Brother Lawrence's death, were never seen by me until this December, when the photographically reproduced pages from the British Library lay upon my desk, so far from Paris and 1693. James Cook was not yet born. Tasman, a few years before Lawrence found his own great landfall, had seen afar a 'high land, uplifted'. He named it New Zealand.

It is from that text, ancient in typeface, smudged a little where the printer, without consistency, lapsed into italics for direct quotation, that the following translation has been made. The Abbé Joseph De Beaufort was responsible for giving Lawrence's fragments to the world. He must, in recognition of this debt, be forgiven for some over-zealous intrusions. His 'Eulogy' is omitted. It contains quotations, but none not reproduced in the other sections . . .

In point of fact we know little about our Brother. He was born Nicholas Herman at Héremini in Lorraine, and became a soldier, probably while still in his 'teens. During a Swedish incursion, he was wounded near the small town of Rambervilliers, and left the army, probably with a permanent disability. He found employment as a footman, not, on his own testimony, a very successful one. What followed is obscure.

We should be glad to know what influences crossed his path after his early conversion at the age of eighteen, and who it was that led him into that deep dealing with God, from which all his subsequent experience derived, but we are told nothing. It was in middle life, but at what age precisely is not certain, that he was received as a lay brother into the order of the 'Discalced Carmelites', well-named from Elijah's retreat. In the following pages, the adjective has been rendered 'Barefoot', but in more severe climates, the brothers were allowed sandals and even socks. It was at this time, after four years of traumatic stress, that Brother Lawrence after an act of complete submission to God, began that development of his special way of life – 'the Practice of the Presence of God'. There is nothing more biographical to add, save for a few details emerging from what he has left recorded, and what was written about him.

The Doctrine

'Brother Lawrence was a mystic . . .' says one dictionary of biography. Is this true? Need he be classified and labelled? It is true that his experience of God was direct and immediate, but are not both words true of all Christian experience? Lawrence knew nothing of the trances, visions and other psycho-physical manifestations associated with mysticism. If he knew 'ecstasy' it was no more than 'the joy of the Lord' of the New Testament, the natural outflow of a soul given over to God.

To be useful a term must have its limits and restrictions, and that remark applies to mysticism in religious terminology. All religions, Jewish and Christian included, manifest mystical phenomena, if by that is meant a keen and salutary awareness of God. Psalm Twenty-Three is a prime example. God the shepherd guides and defends. God the host sets his own at table with him, a concept which appealed to Brother Lawrence. He twice refers to such heavenly banqueting.

'Abide in me,' Christ commanded. Those chapters of John's Gospel which follow the party's leaving of the 'upper room', contain words probably spoken in the Temple court, whither the Lord resorted to postpone his arrest for an hour. A sculptured vine adorned the Temple gate, old symbol of Israel. It shone white, set forth with shadow, in the Paschal moon, and Christ spoke of the union of stock and branches, of fruitfulness 'in him', and of the strength of the indwelling Spirit. Is this mysticism, or plain Christianity?

'Abide with me', and Brother Lawrence did no more and no less. He ever stressed the vital power of faith, the key to all his practice and divine awareness. 'Abiding' is a practice of faith. Godet defines it as 'that continuous act whereby we lay aside all that which we might derive from our own strength to draw all from Christ by faith'. The practice of God's presence, the unbroken attitude of mind which envisages God within, the hearer of all speech, the monitor of all thoughts, the judge of all actions, is precisely 'abiding in Christ'. I knew Godet's definition in 1924, and Brother Lawrence's appeal to me was the simple manner by which he brought the doctrine down to common life.

It is not difficult to understand, in spite of the attempt to reduce it all to formula and doctrine in the 'Spiritual Principles'. Even the 'simple gaze' of that brief treatise finds its place among the expressions of personal piety, common in the language of all kinds of Christians – 'Turn your eyes upon Jesus', for example, 'Gaze full on his wonderful face' . . . Or such words as:

> *Oh the peace which fills my soul*
> *Sitting at the feet of Jesus . . .*

This is my abiding place
Looking upwards to his face . . .

Or even:

In a love which cannot cease,
I am his and he is mine.

Emotion cannot be leached from worship, and the language of human love is naturally called upon to provide the language of devotion. It is precisely here that delicacy of taste and the mind's control must oversee, refine and temper the soul's devotions.

Brother Lawrence will not be found to transgress such limits and guidelines. A calm common sense infuses his spirituality. That, I think, was what I sensed as a young Christian. My faith was warm, but there was enough of the cool academic in me to see the perils of emotion too uninhibited in the exercises of the soul. Lawrence caught my attention. Perhaps he still has much to give. This, then, is a small attempt to introduce an old friend.

PART ONE

The Conversations with Brother Lawrence

Translator's Note

In this translation the conversations are placed first, and are followed by the letters, although that is not the order of the original publications. The conversations* and the letters contain the real substance of what Frère Laurent had to say. How complete and unedited his surviving writings are it is impossible to say. Consider the complicated and highly mystical passage in the first paragraph of the second conversation. It is difficult to believe that his questioner did not receive loaded questions, stemming from some mystical source of contemporary speculation. Brother Lawrence was probably too simple and direct to be serious about such fine distinctions as that drawn between 'receiving God' and 'receiving God's gifts'. It might seem, that, as quickly as politeness allowed, Lawrence turned to the familiar simplicities of his way of life. They must speak for themselves.

* Which cover a period of fifteen months.

Conversations with Brother Lawrence

Conversation One

The Third of August, 1666

The day I first saw Brother Lawrence he told me that God had granted him extraordinary grace in his conversion at the age of eighteen years. . . One day in winter, while looking at a tree stripped of its leaves, and reflecting that after a time its leaves would appear again and then flowers and fruits, he received a lofty view of the providence and the power of God which has never been effaced from his soul. This view drew him altogether from the world, and gave him such a love for God that he was unable to say whether it had increased during the span of forty years since he had received this grace.

He said that he had been footman to Monsieur de Fuibert, treasurer of the Exchequer, and was a big heavy-handed fellow who broke everything. He had sought entry to a monastery thinking that there he would be made to smart for his acts of clumsiness and mistakes, and in this way offer up his life and happiness, but that God had disappointed him because he had found there nothing but contentment. That often made him say to God: 'You have deceived me.'

We should, he said, fix ourselves firmly in the presence of God by conversing all the time with him.

A shameful course it would be to abandon his fellowship to give thought to trifles. We should feed our soul with a lofty conception of God and from that derive great joy in being his. We should put life into our faith. It was a pitiable condition that we had so little faith. Instead of taking it for our rule of living, people gratified themselves with petty acts of devotion which varied from day to day. This path of faith, he said, was the spirit of the Church, and it was enough to take us to a high perfection.

We should give ourselves utterly to God in pure abandonment, in temporal and spiritual matters alike, and find contentment in the doing of his will, whether he takes us through sufferings or consolations. It must be all the same to one who is truly given over to him. There must be faithfulness in those times of dryness by which God tries our love for him. There it is that we make our good acts of surrender and abandonment to him. A single such act often brings much progress on the way.

He said that amid the miseries and sins of which he heard every day, he was not astonished at them, but, on the contrary, surprised there were not yet more, in view of the wickedness of which the sinner is capable. He prayed for the sinner, he said, but knowing that God could apply the remedy when he would, he was not disturbed about it overmuch.

To reach the self-abandonment to God he would desire of us, it behoves us to watch with care all the movements of the soul which interfere with spiritual concerns as well as with those of a grosser kind. God gives illumination for this to those who have the genuine desire to be his. And if I had this purpose, he said, he was at my disposal when I would. Without it, I must not come to see him again.

Conversation Two

The Twenty-Eighth of September, 1666

He said that he was always ruled by love, with no other interest, without concerning himself about whether he would be lost or saved. But having taken as the end of all his actions, to do them all for the love of God, he was well satisfied therewith. He was happy, he said, to pick up a straw from the ground for the love of God, seeking him alone, purely, and nothing else, not even his gifts. This attitude of soul caused God to give him endless gifts of grace; but often in taking the fruit of these graces, that is to say the love born of them, he found it necessary to reject their savour, saying that all of it was not God himself at all, since one knew by faith that he was infinitely greater, and quite different from that which one felt. In this transaction there came about between God and the soul a wondrous struggle – God giving, and the soul denying that it was God which it was receiving. In this struggle the soul by faith was as strong and stronger than God, since he was never able so to give that the soul was not able to continue denying that what he had given was himself.

The ecstasy and rapture were only those of a soul which took pleasure in the gift, instead of rejecting it, and going on to God beyond his gift. Beyond the wonderment one should not allow oneself to be carried away, God being, for all that, in control. And God, he said, would repay so readily and so liberally for everything one did for him, that at times he had wished he could hide from God that which he did for the love of him, so that, receiving no reward, he might have the joy of doing something for God and God alone.

He had been, he said, in enormous anguish of soul, believing certainly that he was lost, and all the people in the world would not have been able to take this conviction from him. But he reasoned this way about it: 'I took on a monk's life only for the love of God. I have sought only to live for him. Whether I be lost or saved it is my desire to go on living purely for the love of God. This good, at least, I shall have that, right until death, I shall do what lies in me to love him.' This anguish had lasted four years during which he had suffered much. Since then he had worried neither about Paradise nor Hell; all his life had been freedom and unbroken rejoicing. He placed his sins, he said, between God and himself as though to say to him that he deserved none of his favours. That did not prevent God from overwhelming him with them, and God at times took him as by the hand and led him before all the heavenly court to exhibit the wretch to whom he took pleasure to grant his grace.

A little perseverance, he said, was needed at first to form the habit of conversing all the time with God and referring all actions to him. However, after a little care one felt stirred by his love without any trouble. He quite expected, after the good times which God gave him, that he should have his turn, and share in troubles and sufferings, but he was not disturbed about it, knowing well that, since he could do nothing for himself, God would not be lacking to give him the strength to endure them. When he set himself the task of putting some virtue into practice, he would address himself to God, saying: 'God, I should not be able to do that unless you enabled me to do it', and then he was given immediately the strength to do it and more besides.

When he had fallen short, he said, he would do nothing else but confess his shortcoming and say to God: 'I should never do anything else if you left it to me to do it. It is yours to prevent me from falling and to set right that which is not well.' After that he concerned himself no more over his fault. We ought to act very simply with God, speaking familiarly with him, and asking him for help in situations as they arise. God would not fail to give it as he had often experienced.

He had been sent off a few days earlier to Burgundy for stocks of wine, a painful task for him as he had no aptitude for business, was lame in one leg, and could only get about the boat by rolling himself over the casks. He did not, however, trouble himself about this, no more than about his whole purchase of wine. He told God that it was his business, after which he found that everything worked out and worked out well. He had been sent to Auvergne the year before on a similar errand. He could not say how the business worked out. It was not he who managed it and it turned out very well.

It was just the same in the kitchen to which he had a strong natural aversion, but he trained himself to do everything there for the love of God, and on praying at every juncture for his grace to do his work, he had found it very easy during the fifteen years he was thus employed. At the moment he was in the cobbler's workshop, and was most happy there, but he was ready to leave this employment like the rest, always making himself do small things for the love of God.

The time of prayer was, he said, in no way different for him than any other. He would observe his times of withdrawal when the Father Prior bade him do so, but he neither wanted nor asked for them, because his most demanding work did not divert him from God.

Knowing that he must love God in all things, and striving to fulfil this obligation, he had no need of a director, but certainly of a confessor to receive absolution for the faults of which he was guilty. Of such he was very well aware, and was not at all put out by them. He would confess them to God, and make no plea to him to excuse them, and afterwards would return in peace to his common business of love and adoration.

In his troubles he had not consulted anyone, but with the light of faith, knowing that God only was present, he was satisfied to deal with only him, come what may, and he was willing thus to lose all for the love of God with which he was content. Thoughts spoil everything. All evil begins there. We must take care to set them aside as soon as we observe them not to be necessary for the task of the moment or for our salvation, so that we can begin again our converse with God, wherein is our only good. He had often passed all his set time for prayer in these preliminaries, setting thoughts aside and falling into them again. He had never been able to undertake the time of prayer by rule as the others did. At first, however, he had used spoken prayer for some time but afterwards the habit passed and he could not say why.

He had asked, he said, to remain a novice always, not believing that one would want to receive him into the order and unable to imagine that his two years had gone. He was not sturdy enough to ask God for acts of penitence, nor did he want them, but he well knew that he truly deserved them, and that when God should send them he would also give him the grace to endure them. All penitential acts and other exercises served only to forward union with God through love, and after having deeply pondered this, he had concluded that it was a shorter way to go straight there by a continual exercise of love, and doing everything for the love of God.

A great distinction must be made between the actions of the understanding and those of the will. The former signified little, the latter everything. All we have to do is love, and be happy in God. Though we should perform all possible acts of penitence, if they were void of love, they would not serve to blot out a single sin. Without anxiety we should expect the pardon which comes from the Blood of Jesus Christ, striving only to love him with all our heart. God seemed to choose those who had been the greatest sinners to bestow upon them his greatest favours, rather than those who had dwelt in innocence, for this is what best showed his loving-kindness.

He gave thought neither to death, nor his sins, nor Paradise nor Hell, but only to do small things for the love of God. Great things, he said, he was not able to do. That done, there would come upon him only what God should will, and of that he had no concern. Though he should be flayed alive, it would be nothing compared with what he had suffered spiritually, or with the great joys he had often had. Thus he was concerned about nothing, feared nothing, and asked nothing, save that he might not offend God.

He told me that he had few scruples, for, said he, 'when I feel convicted of a fault I do not deny it and I say: That is the way with me. That is all I can do . . . When I have not failed, I give due thanks for it to God, and confess that it comes from him.'

Conversation Three

The Twenty-Second of November, 1666

He told me that the foundation of the spiritual life in him had been a lofty idea and conception of God by faith. Once he had firmly grasped this, he had no other care than to cast faithfully aside from the beginning every other thought, so as to do all that he did for the love of God. When, on occasion, he went a long time without thinking about him, he did not trouble himself, but after confessing his wretchedness to God, he returned to him with all the more confidence for having sensed such wretchedness in thus forgetting him. The confidence which we have in God greatly honours him and attracts great favours. It is impossible, not only that God should deceive, but even that he should long leave to suffer a soul utterly abandoned to him, and resolved to endure all for him.

He had reached the point, he said, where he thought only of God, and when something else or some temptation arose, he sensed their coming, and from the experience he had of God's prompt aid, it happened at times that he let them advance, and at the right moment called on God. They were gone forthwith. From the same experience, when he had some mundane business to do, he gave no thought to it in advance, but, when it was time for action, he found in God, as in a clear mirror, what was needful to be done at the present moment. For some time he had acted in this fashion, not anticipating trouble. Before this experience of God's prompt help in his affairs, he devoted foresight to them. Nor did he keep in mind the things which he did, and gave small attention even in the midst of doing them. Rising from table he did not know what he had eaten, but in accordance with the simplicity of his outlook, he did all for the love of God, giving him due thanks for directing what he did, and doing numberless other things, but all very simply, and in a manner which kept him firm in the loving presence of God.

When outward occupation called his mind a little from thinking on God, there would come to him from God's part some reminder which invested his soul, giving it some stronger sense of God, warming and firing it at times so strongly that he cried aloud, singing and dancing as vigorously as a madman. He was even more at one with God in his common activities, than when he turned from them for the formal activities of retreat, from which he would return to common life only with much dryness.

He expected to have in the course of time some great affliction of body or mind, and that the worst that could happen to him would be to lose that sense of God which he had so long had, but the loving-kindness of God assured him that he would not completely abandon him, and that he would give him strength to bear such evil as he might allow to befall him. With that he feared nothing, and had no need to consult anyone about his soul. When he had desired to do so, he had always come away more perplexed. Being willing to die and to lose himself for the love of God, he had no foreboding. Complete abandonment to God was the sure way, and one on which there was always light to travel.

It was needful at the beginning to act faithfully and renounce self, but after that there were only unutterable joys. In difficulties one had only to turn to Jesus Christ and ask for his grace, after which all became easy. One could become entangled in acts of penitence and special devotions, leaving love which is the end. This is obvious to see in what people do, and the reason why one sees so little solid virtue. It requires no skill nor knowledge to go to God, but only a heart resolute to turn to him, and for him, and to love only him.

Conversation Four

The Twenty-Fifth of November, 1667

Brother Lawrence often spoke to me with great fervour and frankness of his way of approaching God. Of this I have already taken some note. He told me that it all amounted to one good act of renunciation of everything which we recognise does not lead to God, in order to habituate ourselves to an unbroken converse with him without mystery or artificiality. It is only necessary to realise that God is intimately present within us, to turn at every moment to him and ask for his help, recognise his will in all things doubtful, and to do well all that which we clearly see he requires of us, offering what we do to him before we do it, and giving thanks for having done it afterwards. In this unbroken communion one is continually preoccupied with praising, worshipping and loving God for his infinite acts of loving-kindness and perfection.

We should in all confidence ask for his grace without regard to what we think, relying only on the infinite merits of our Lord. God never fails to offer his grace at every juncture. He perceived this keenly, and said that he never failed save when he wandered from the company of God, or had forgotten to ask for his help.

When we are in doubt, God will never fail to give light when we have no other plan than to please him and to act in love for him. Our sanctification does not depend upon some alteration in what we do, but in doing for God what we commonly do for ourselves. It was lamentable, he said, to see how many people were set on doing certain things which they did only most imperfectly because of their many human preoccupations, always mistaking the means for the end. He found the best means of drawing near to God was through the common tasks which obedience laid down for him, purging them as far as lies in us from every human ingredient, and performing them all for the pure love of God.

It was, he said, enormous self-deception to believe that the time of prayer must be different from any other. We are equally bound to be one with God by what we do in times of action as by the time of prayer at its special hour. His prayer was simply the presence of God, his soul unconscious of all else but love. But apart from such times he discovered scarcely any difference, keeping himself always near to God praising and blessing him with all his might, passing his life in unbroken joy, yet hoping that God would give him something to suffer when he should grow stronger. We should once for all, he said, trust ourselves to God, abandon ourselves to him alone, knowing that he would not deceive us. We must not grow weary in doing little things for the love of God, who looks not to the greatness of the deed, but to the love. Some failure at the start should not dismay us. Habit comes finally, and that produces the action without our thinking about it, and with wondrous joy.

He said that only faith, hope and love had to be nourished to become utterly dedicated to the will of God. All the rest was unimportant. One should pause there only as if upon a bridge, to be quickly crossed on the way to lose oneself by confidence and love in the final goal. All things are possible to him who believes, more to him who hopes, and still more to him who practises and goes on practising these three virtues. The goal which we must set before ourselves is to be in this life the most perfect worshippers of God possible, as we hope to be through all eternity.

When we undertake the spiritual life we should consider fundamentally what manner of people we are. Then we shall discover ourselves to be worthy of all contempt, unworthy of the name of Christian, subject to all sorts of distress and numberless mischances which disturb us, and make us uneven in our health, moods, dispositions within and outside ourselves, in a word people whom God must bring low by boundless troubles and toils within and without. After that should we be amazed if troubles, temptations, opposition and contradiction of all kinds befall us in society? On the contrary we must submit to them and endure them as long as God shall please as experiences which are for our good. The higher the perfection to which a soul aspires the more dependent it is upon grace.

PART TWO

The Letters of Brother Lawrence

Translator's Note

The letters, half of which are dated, cover a period of almost nine years. Six of the sixteen are dated within two years of his death in February, 1691, four of them in the last four months of life, and two in the last month.

Some are fairly obviously complete, with formal beginning and end. Others begin at some point considered relevant, and one of them acknowledges the omission of private details.

There is no noticeable difference between the Lawrence of the Conversations, and the Lawrence revealed in the letters of a generation later. He has continued in the one practical message he had to teach. If there is anything new it is only his mild distaste for human medicine revealed in the closing letters to the suffering senior nun, a distaste which will be shared by any who look into the shocking therapy and pharmacology of the day – the treatment, for example, and the physic which Louis himself endured at the hands of the royal doctors in his last painful illnesses.

It is a great loss that Lawrence's correspondents did not keep and make available more examples of a probably wider and more varied collection, though, to be sure, some could have heeded the stringent directions which introduce the Twelfth Letter.

Here, at any rate, is Lawrence himself, probably

33

unedited, simple, direct, a little monotonous, and sometimes too involved in his phraseology, but showing just a touch of the unadorned style of the best writing of that great century. There seems to be only one really awkward or confused sentence. And he was, at the end, a sick man. His last written words were of a prayer soon to be answered.

Letters of Brother Lawrence

First Letter

To The Reverend Mother N

My Reverend Mother,

I take this opportunity to share with you the thoughts of one of our community on the wonderful effects and continual help he has received from the practice of the presence of God. Let us both profit from them.

You will know that his chief care over the forty years that he has been in a religious order, has been always to be in God's presence and to do nothing, to say nothing and to think nothing, which might displease him, with nothing else in mind but the pure love of him, love of which he deserves infinitely more.

At the present time he is so accustomed to this divine presence that he receives from it continual help on all manner of occasions. For some thirty years past his soul revels in joys so unbroken, and so strong that sometimes, to control them and prevent their being outwardly visible, he is constrained to manifest juvenile behaviour which smacks rather of folly than devotion.

If at times he is a little withdrawn from this divine presence, God immediately makes him aware of it in his soul to recall him, an experience which he often has in the midst of mundane occupation. His reply is a prompt obedience to these inner appeals, by a lifting of the heart, or by a sweet and loving gaze or by some words which love discovers in these encounters – as for example: 'My God, here I am, all yours'; 'Lord, fashion me according to thy heart.' And then it appears to him that he experiences indeed that the God of love, satisfied with these few words, returns to rest and to repose in the very centre of his soul. The consciousness of these things makes him so aware that God is ever in the depths of his being, that he can conceive no doubt about it, whatever he does and whatever happens to him.

Judge from this, my Reverend Mother, what contentment and satisfaction he enjoys, conscious, as he is, of so great a treasure within him. He is no longer anxious about finding it; he has not the trouble of seeking it; he is free to take what he pleases of it.

He often deplores our blindness, and is always complaining that we are to be pitied for being satisfied with so little. God, he says, has boundless treasures to give us, and a moment's sense of devotion is enough for us. We are blind who so bind the hands of God, and we stem the abundance of his grace. When he finds a soul imbued with living faith, into it he pours grace on grace, a flowing stream, as it were, which, checked in its proper course, and finding a new outlet spreads wide with force, abundantly.

Yes, we often check this torrent by the small regard we have for it. Let us check it no more, my dear Mother; let us return into ourselves, break down this dam, make open way for grace, and make up for lost time. Perhaps we have little time left to live. Death is not far away. Let us be alert for it. One dies but once.

Again, let us return into ourselves. Time presses. There is no postponement. Each man is responsible for himself. I believe you have taken such effective measures that you will not be taken by surprise. For this I praise you for that is life. However, we must go on working, for in the life of the spirit not to go on is to lose ground. Those who have the mind of the Holy Spirit, sail on, even when they are asleep. If the small ship of our soul is still beaten by the winds and the storm, let us awaken the Lord who sleeps in it, and he will soon calm the sea.

I have taken the liberty, my very dear Mother, of sharing these thoughts with you, to set them face to face with your own. They will serve to relight and kindle them, if by mischance (which God forbid, for that would be bad indeed) they should be growing cold, be it but a little. Let us then recall ourselves, both you and me, to our first ardours, and profit by the example and the thoughts of this monk, little known to the world, but known to God and deeply cherished by him. I will petition him for you. And do you pray most urgently for him who is in our Lord, My Reverend Mother

Yours etc.

From Paris
June 1, 1682

Second Letter

To the Reverend Mother N

My Reverend and Most Honoured Mother,
I have today received two books and a letter from Sister N, who is preparing to make her vows, and

asks in that regard for the prayers of your holy community, and especially yours. She impresses me as having in them a very great, indeed singular trust, so do not disappoint her. Ask God that she may make her sacrifice in the light only of his love, and with a firm resolve to be God's alone. I will send you one of these books which deals with the 'presence of God'. Therein, to my mind, lies the whole life of the spirit, and it seems to me that, in its proper practice, one soon becomes spiritual.

To that end I know the heart must be empty of all else, for God wishes to be its only possessor, and since he cannot be its only possessor without emptying it of all that is not himself, so too he cannot act therein or do his will.

There is not in the world a way of life more sweet, nor more delightful than continual converse with God. Those only who practise it, and savour it, can understand it. And yet I do not counsel you to act on this motive, for it is not consolations we must seek in this practice. Let us act on a principle of love, and because God wills it.

If I were a preacher, I should preach nothing else but the practice of the presence of God. If I were a director, I should recommend it to everyone, so much do I believe it essential and even easy.

Ah, if we knew the need we have for the grace and favour of God we should never lose the vision of it for even a second. Believe me, and from this moment make a holy and firm resolution never willingly to depart from it, and to live the rest of your days in this holy presence, reft, for the love of him, if he so wills, of the consolations of heaven and of earth. Put your hand to the task. If you do it as it should be done, be assured that you will soon see the results. I shall assist you with my prayers, poor though they are. I commend myself very urgently to yours, and to those of your holy community, as I am to all of them, and to you especially,

Yours etc.

Undated.

Third Letter

To the Same Person

My Reverend and Most Honoured Mother,

I have received from Mlle N the rosaries which you sent me by her. I am amazed that you did not tell me what you thought about the book which I sent you, and which you must have received. Practise it with determination in your declining years. Better late than never.

I cannot understand how women in religious communities can live content without the practice of the presence of God. For my part I keep myself apart with him, at the depth and centre of my soul as much as I am able, and when I am thus with him I fear nothing. But the smallest deviation is a hell for me. This exercise does not destroy the body, but it is pertinent from time to time – even frequently – to deprive it of many small consolations, even innocent and permissible ones, for God does not suffer that a soul which desires to be entirely his, should receive other consolations than with him – which is more than reasonable.

For all that, I do not say that one must suffer undue inconvenience. One must serve God in a holy liberty and do one's work faithfully without distress or anxiety, calling the soul gently and quietly back to God so soon as we find it drawn away from him. It is, however, needful to put all one's confidence in God and to unburden oneself of all other cares, even of many personal devotions which, very good though they may be, we inadvisedly take upon ourselves.

After all they are only means to reach the end. Thus, when by this exercise of the presence of God, we are with him who is our end, it is useless to go back to the means. We can continue with him our communion of love, abiding in his holy presence, now by an act of worship, praise, or aspiration, now by an act of self-offering, the giving of thanks, and in all the ways our spirit will know how to devise.

Do not be discouraged by the distaste you will feel in your human nature. You must buffet yourself. At the onset one often feels that it is a waste of time, but you must go on, and determine to persevere therein to death in spite of all the difficulties. I commend myself to the prayers of your holy community and especially to your own.

I am in Our Lord
Your etc.

Paris
    November 3, 1685

Fourth Letter

To Madame N

Madame,

I am truly sorry for you. If you could leave the management of your affairs to Monsieur and Madame N, and give yourself entirely to prayer to God, you would begin a revolution. He does not ask much of us – an occasional remembrance, a small act of worship, now to beg his grace, at times to offer him our distresses, at another time to render thanks for the favours he has given, and which he gives in the midst of your labours, to find consolation with him as often as you can. At table and in the midst of conversation, lift your heart at times towards him. The smallest remembrance will always please him. It is not needful at such times to cry out loud. He is nearer to us than we think.

It is not needful always to be in church to be with God. We can make a chapel of our heart, to which we can from time to time withdraw to have gentle, humble, loving communion with him. Everyone is able to have these familiar conversations with God, some more, some less – he knows our capabilities. Let us make a start. Perhaps he only waits for us to make one whole-hearted resolve. Courage! We have but a short time to live. You are almost sixty-four years of age. As for me, I am almost eighty. Let us live and die with God. Sufferings will be sweet and pleasant to us when we are with him, and without him the greatest pleasures will be only cruel torture. May he be blessed in all. Amen.

Grow accustomed, then, little by little thus to worship him, to ask for his grace, to offer him your heart from time to time in the course of the day, amid your labours, at any time you can. Do not fetter yourself by rules or special forms of worship. Act in faith, with love, and with humility. You can assure Monsieur and Madame De N and Mademoiselle N of my poor prayers. I am their servant and yours in Our Lord,

Brother etc.

Undated but
    probably 1690

Fifth Letter

To the Reverend Father N

My Reverend Father,
    Not finding my way of life in books, and although I have no difficulties about it, for greater assurance, I should like to know what you think about my present condition.
    Not many days ago in a personal discussion with a man of piety, it was remarked to me that the spiritual life was a way of grace, which begins with a servile fear, increases with the hope of eternal life and is consummated in pure love, and that in the process there are different stages whereby this happy consummation is attained.

I have in no way followed these steps. On the contrary, by what allure I do not know, they filled me at first with fear. The result was that, when I entered the order, I formed the resolution to give myself completely to God in satisfaction for my sins, and for the love of him to renounce everything apart from him.

During these years, the common preoccupation of my prayers was thoughts of death, judgment, Hell, Paradise, and my sins. So I continued for some years, applying myself carefully for the rest of the day, and even during my work, to the practice of the presence of God, whom I looked upon as always near me, often even in the depths of my heart. This gave me so exalted a notion of God that faith alone was able to satisfy me on this matter.

Gradually I came to do the same during my prayers, and this gave me continually great comfort and consolation. That is how I began. I shall tell you, however, that during the first ten years I suffered much. The apprehension I had of not belonging to God as I should have wished, my past sins always present before my eyes, and the goodness of God to me, were the material and the source of my woes. During all this time I often fell, straightway rising to my feet again. It seemed to me that man, reason, and even God were against me, and that faith alone was for me. I was sometimes distressed that it all flowed from my presumption, that I was thinking to be immediately at the point which others reached with toil; at other times I thought I was damning myself gratuitously, that there was no salvation at all for me.

When I thought no more than to end my days in these troubles and anxieties (which in no way diminished the trust I had in God, and which served only to increase my faith) I found myself suddenly changed, and my soul, which up until then was always in distress, experienced a deep inner peace, as if it was in its centre and in a place of rest.

Since that time, I work before God simply in faith, with humility and with love, and I apply myself to do nothing, say nothing and think nothing which can displease him. I hope that, when I have done all I can, he will do with me according to his will.

I cannot express to you what goes on in me now. I sense no distress nor any doubt about my state. I have no other will but God's will, which I seek to fulfil in all things, and to which I am so committed that I would not wish to pick up a piece of straw without his command, and for any other motives than pure love of him.

I have abandoned all my forms of worship, and those prayers which are not obligatory, and I do nothing else but abide in his holy presence, and I do this by a simple attentiveness and an habitual, loving turning of my eyes on him. This I should call the actual presence of God, or to put it better, a wordless and secret conversation between the soul and God which no longer ends. It often gives me such deep feelings of inner (even outer) contentment and joy, that to restrain them and prevent their visible manifestation, I am induced to act childishly in a manner which smacks more of folly than of worship.

Indeed, my Reverend Father, I can in no way doubt that my soul has been with God these past thirty years. I omit many matters lest I should weary you, but I think however, it is appropriate to set out for you how I look upon myself before God whom I regard as my king.

I regard myself as the most wretched of all men, ragged with sores, full of malodorous things and guilty of all manner of crimes against his king. Touched by a live repentance, I confess all my evil deeds to him, I implore his pardon, and give myself over into his hands to do with me as he will. This king, full of goodness and mercy, far from chastising me, embraces me lovingly, makes me eat at his table, serves me with his own hands, gives me the keys to his treasures, and treats me just as if I were his favourite. He talks with me and has ceaseless pleasure in my company in a thousand thousand ways. He does not speak of my pardon or taking away my one-time way of life, though I beseech him to do with me according to his heart, and see myself as ever more weak and wretched, yet more cherished by God. That is how I sometimes think of myself in his holy presence.

My commonest attitude is this simple attentiveness, an habitual, loving turning of my eyes to God, to whom I often find myself bound with more happiness and gratification than that which a babe enjoys clinging to its nurse's breast. So, if I dare use this expression, I should be glad to describe this condition as 'the breasts of God', for the inexpressible happiness I savour and experience there.

If at times I turn aside from it by necessity or weakness, I am forthwith recalled by urgings of the heart so sweet and so entrancing that I am at a loss to describe them. I beg you, my Reverend Father, to consider rather my great imperfections on which you are fully informed, than these great favours with which God blesses my soul, all unworthy and ungrateful though I be.

As for my hours of regular prayer, they are only a

continuation of this same exercise. Sometimes I think of myself as a piece of stone before its sculptor, from which he intends to make a statue. Setting myself thus before God, I beg him to shape his perfect image in my soul, and to make me exactly like him.

At other times, as soon as I apply myself, I feel all my spirit and all my soul lifted, without solicitude or striving and it abides, as though uplifted and firmly placed in God as in its centre and abiding place.

I know that some folk call this condition slothfulness, deception and self-love. I admit that there is a sort of holy slothfulness, a blessed self-love, if the soul were capable of such, in this condition, since, indeed, the soul, in this repose, cannot be concerned with those actions of past time which were its support, but which would now rather harm than aid it.

But I cannot allow it to be called deception, because the soul which thus enjoys God, desires only him. If it is deception in me, it is for God to remedy it, that he may do his will with me. I want only him, and to be all his. However, I should be obliged if you would let me know what you think, for as I especially respect your Reverence, I defer much to your opinion.

I am in Our Lord, my Reverend Father,
Your etc.

Undated.

Sixth Letter

To the Reverend Mother N

My Reverend and Most Honoured Mother,

My prayers, of little value though they be, shall not fail you. That I have promised, and I shall keep my word. How happy we should be if we could find the treasure of which the Gospel speaks. The rest would seem nothing to us. Since it is boundless, the more we dig, the more wealth we find there. Let us ceaselessly search for it. Let us not grow weary until we have found it . . .

Finally, my Reverend Mother, I do not know what will happen to me. It seems that peace, love, and rest of soul come to me while I am asleep. If I were capable of suffering, there would be none for me to have, and if I were allowed, I should gladly submit to that of Purgatory, where I believe I shall suffer in satisfaction for my sins. I know not what God lays up for me. I live in quietness so great that I fear nothing. What can I fear when I am with him, and there I keep myself as I am able? May he be blessed by all. Amen.

Yours etc.

(Undated and incomplete.
Some personal matters in
the middle omitted by the
collector of the letters
or by Madame N)

Seventh Letter

To Madame N

Madame,

We have a God infinitely good, and who knows what we need. I have always believed that he would bring you to ultimate affliction. He will come in his good time, and when you least expect him. Hope in him more than ever. Thank him for the favours that he shows you, particularly for the strength and the patience he is giving you in your afflictions – an evident sign of the care he has for you. Be comforted therefore in him, and thank him for everything.

I admire, also, the strength and courage of Monsieur De N. God has given him a good disposition and a good will, but there is still in it a little of the world, and much of youth. I hope that the affliction which God has sent him will serve as a salutary medicine for him, and will make him turn to his own inner person. It is an opportunity to induce him to put all his trust in the one who is always by his side. Let him think of him as often as he can, above all in the greatest perils.

A small lifting of the heart suffices, a small remembrance of God, a movement of the heart's worship, though in haste and with sword in hand, are prayers, which, brief though they may be, are yet most pleasing to God, and, very far from making those engaged in battle lose their courage, in the most dangerous moments they make them brave. Let him remember them, then, as often as he will, let him, little by little, habituate himself to this small but holy discipline. No one sees it, and nothing is more easy than to repeat often throughout the day these small acts of worship in the heart. Recommend to him, please, to remember God, in the way I explain for him here, as often as he can. It is a way most fitting and most necessary for a soldier, daily exposed to dangers to his life, and often to his salvation. I hope that God will aid him and all his family, to whom I send greetings. I am, in all ways,

Your most humble etc.

October 12, 1688

Eighth Letter

My Reverend and Most Honoured Mother,
    You tell me nothing new. You are not the only one to be troubled by your thoughts. Our mind is always given to roving, but since the will is the mistress of all our powers it should recall the mind, and bear it to God, its final end.
    When the mind which has not been early subdued, has developed some bad habits of wandering and inattention, they are difficult to overcome, and they draw us commonly, in spite of ourselves, to earthly things.
    I believe that the cure for this is to confess all our faults and to humble ourselves before God. I do not advise you do much talking at prayer, for much talking is often an occasion for wandering Hold yourself before God like a poor dumb person, or a paralytic at a rich man's gate. Give your attention to

49

keeping your mind in the presence of the Lord. If it wanders and withdraws at times, do not be disturbed. To trouble the mind serves more often to distract than to recall it. The will must call it back quietly. If you persevere in this, God will have pity on you.

One way to recall the mind easily during the time of prayer, and to keep it more at rest, is not to allow it to strive too much during the day. It must be kept strictly in the presence of God. Being accustomed to remember him from time to time, it will be easy to remain quiet during your prayers, or at least to recall the mind from its straying.

I have spoken to you at length in my other letters of the benefits to be found in this practice of God's presence. Let us give ourselves seriously to it, and pray for one another. I commend myself also to the prayers of Sister N, and the Reverend Mother N, and I am for all of you, in Our Lord,

Your very humble etc.

Undated.

Ninth Letter

To the Same Person

Here is the reply to the letter I have received from our good Sister N. Be so kind as to give it to her. She seems to me to be full of goodwill, but she would like to go faster than grace. We cannot become holy all at once. I commend her to you. We must help one another by our advice, and more by our good example. I shall be glad to receive news of her from time to time, and whether she is very ardent or very obedient.

Let us often have in mind, my dear Mother, that our sole business in this life is to please God. What is the total of the rest but foolishness and vanity? We have lived more than forty years in a religious order. Have we used them to love and serve God who in his mercy called us to it, and for this purpose? I am filled with shame and confusion when, on the one hand, I reflect on the great graces which God has bestowed, and ceaselessly goes on bestowing upon me, and, on the other hand, of the ill-use I have made of them, and on my poor progress on the path of perfection.

Since by his mercy he gives us yet a little time, let us begin in earnest, recover lost time, and come back with full trust to this father of loving-kindness, who is always ready lovingly to receive us. Let us renounce, my dear Mother, let us renounce, I say, wholeheartedly, all that is not of him. He deserves infinitely more. Let us think of him unceasingly. Let us put all our trust in him. I have no doubt that we shall soon experience the full effects of doing so, and shall sense the abundance of that grace with which we can do all things, and without which we can only sin.

We cannot avoid the dangers and the reefs of which this life is full, without the real and constant help of God. Let us ask him for it without ceasing. But how can we ask him without being with him? And how can we be with him without often thinking of him? And how can we often think of him without forming a holy habit of doing so? You will tell me that

I am always saying the same thing to you. It is true, and I do not know a better and easier means than that. And since I practise no other, I urge it upon everybody. We must know before we love, and to know God we must often think of him. And when we love him we shall think of him all the more, for our heart is where our treasure is. Let us often think about it, and think about it well.

Your very humble etc.

March 28, 1689

Tenth Letter

To Madame N

I had great difficulty in making up my mind to write to Monsieur De N. I do so only because you and Madame de N desire it. Be so kind then, to address the letter and to send it to him. I am well pleased with the trust you have in God. It is my wish that he increase it more and more. We shall not be able to have too much in a friend so good and faithful, who will never fail us in this world or the next.

If Monsieur De N can profit from the loss he has had, and places all his trust in God, he will soon give him another friend more powerful and better intentioned. He deals with hearts as he wills. Perhaps there was too much human attachment to him whom he has lost. We ought to love our friends, but without prejudice to the love of God who must come first.

Remember, I pray, what I have urged upon you, which is to think often of God, day and night, in all your tasks, in all your religious duties, even in all your amusements. He is always at your side. Do not fail in fellowship with him. You would consider it discourteous to neglect a friend who visited you. Why abandon God and leave him alone? Do not then forget him. Think of him often. Worship him all the time. Live and die with him. That is the Christian's lovely task, in a word, our calling. If we do not know it we must learn it. I will help you therein by my prayers. I am, in our Lord,

Yours etc.

Paris
   October 29, 1689

Eleventh Letter

To the Reverend Mother N

I do not ask God that you should be delivered from your sufferings, but I never cease to ask him to give you the strength and patience to endure them for as long as he sees fit. Find consolation in him who keeps you nailed to the cross. He will free you from it when he thinks that it is right. Happy are they who suffer for him. Grow accustomed thus to suffer. Ask him for strength to suffer all that which he wills, and for as long as he shall judge it to be needful for you. The world does not comprehend these truths, and I am

53

not surprised. They suffer as worldlings do, and not as Christians. They regard sicknesses as Nature's afflictions, and not as demonstrations of God's grace, and that is why they only find there that which is hostile and rough in Nature. But those who look upon them as coming from the hand of God, as the results of his mercy, and as the means which he uses for their salvation, commonly find in them great happiness and real consolation.

I wish that you could believe that God is often nearer to us in our times of sickness and infirmity, than when we are enjoying perfect health. Seek no other medicine than him. To the best of my understanding, he wishes to heal us alone. Put all your trust in him. You will soon see the results. We often delay healing by putting greater trust in remedies than in God.

Some remedies which you use will work only so far as he shall permit. When pains come from God, he alone can heal them. He often leaves us maladies of the body to heal those of the soul. Find consolation in the supreme medicine of souls and bodies too.

I foresee that you will reply that I am very comfortable, that I drink and eat at the table of the Lord. You are right, but do you think it would be a small distress to the greatest criminal in the world to eat at the king's table and to be served by his hands, without, however, being assured of his forgiveness? I think that he would feel the greatest distress, which only confidence in the goodness of his sovereign could assuage. Can I also assure you that whatever happiness I feel in drinking and eating at the king's table, my sins, ever before my eyes, as also the uncertainty of my pardon, are a torment to me – though, in truth, such distress is sweet to me.

Be contented with the state in which God has placed you. However happy you may think me, I envy you. Pains and sufferings will be a Paradise for me, then I shall suffer with God, and the greatest pleasures would be a Hell, if I tasted them without him. All my consolation would be to suffer something for him.

I am soon at the point of going to see God. I mean to render an account to him, for if I have seen God but for a single moment, the pains of Purgatory would be sweet to me, even if they should last to the end of the world. What consoles me in this life is that I see God by faith. And I see him in a way which could at times make me say: 'I no longer believe, but I see.' I experience what faith teaches us, and upon this assurance and practice of faith I shall live and die with him.

Hold fast, then, to God always. It is the one and and only comfort for your ills. I shall beg him to be with you. I greet the Reverend Mother Prioress and commend myself to her holy prayers, as to those of the holy community and your own. I am, in Our Lord,

Your etc.

November 17, 1690

Twelfth Letter

To the Reverend Mother N

My Reverend Mother,

Since you so earnestly desire that I share with you the method I have kept to reach this condition of the presence of God, in which our Lord by his mercy has been pleased to place me, I cannot hide from you that it is with the utmost reluctance that I allow myself to yield to your importunities, and, further, on this condition that you show my letter to no one. If I knew that you felt obliged to show it, all the desire I have for your perfection would not induce me. What I can tell you about it is this:

Having found in many books ways of drawing near to God, and different practices of the spiritual life, I concluded that it would tend to embarrass my mind rather than promote my quest and search, which was only to find a means of being wholly God's. That led me to the resolve to give all for all. Thus, after giving myself wholly to God in satisfaction for my sins, I renounced, for the love of him, everything which was not of him, and began to live as if there were none but I and he in the world. I sometimes thought of myself in his presence as a poor malefactor at the feet of his Judge. At other times I looked on him in my heart as my Father and my God. I worshipped him there as often as I could, holding my spirit in his holy presence, and recalling him to mind as often as I found myself turned aside from him. I had no small trouble with this exercise, which

I carried on in spite of all the difficulties I found in it, without stress or anxiety on those occasions when I turned unwillingly aside from him. I acted thus not less throughout the day than in my set times of prayer, for at all times at every hour and moment, on my busiest occasions, I would banish and thrust from my mind everything calculated to take from me the thought of God.

This, then, my Reverend Mother, has been my common practice since I entered religion. Though I have practised it with much slackness and many imperfections, I have none the less received from it immense advantages. I well know that it is to the mercy and the goodness of the Lord that they must be attributed, since we can do nothing apart from him, and I even less than all the rest. But when we faithfully hold ourselves in his holy presence, thinking of him as always before us, apart from restraining us from offending and doing aught which might displease him, at least willingly, by dint of thinking of him thus, we take the holy liberty of asking him for the gifts of grace of which we stand in need. In fact, by often repeating these 'acts' they become more a matter of habit, and the presence of God becomes, in a way, natural. Join with me, if you please, in thanking him for his great goodness towards me. I can never wonder enough at the number of favours he has bestowed on so miserable a sinner as I am. May he be blessed by all. Amen. I am in Our Lord,

Yours etc.

Undated.

Thirteenth Letter

To the Reverend Mother N

My Good Mother,

If we were well disciplined in the practice of the presence of God, all bodily maladies would be light to us. Often God allows us to suffer a little to purify our soul, and to compel us to abide with him. I cannot understand how a soul that is with God, and desires only him, should be capable of wretchedness. I have enough experience to be convinced of this. Take courage. Offer him ceaselessly your sufferings. Beg him for strength to bear them. Above all make a habit of often holding communion with him. Forget him as little as you can. Worship him in your infirmities. Keep repeating your self-surrender, and in your worst pain ask him humbly and lovingly, like a child his good father, for resignation to his holy will, and the aid of his grace. I will aid you therein by my poor and puny prayers.

God has many ways of drawing us to him, and sometimes conceals himself from us, but the simple faith which will not fail us in time of need, must be our support and the foundation of our trust, which must be all in God.

I do not know what God intends to do with me. My happiness keeps growing. Everyone is suffering, and I, who should be under rigorous discipline, sense joys so unbroken and so great that I have difficulty in restraining them.

I should willingly ask God for a portion of your

sufferings, if I did not know that my weakness is so great that, if he left me for a moment to myself, I should be the most wretched of all creatures. And yet I do not know how he could leave me alone, since faith enables me to touch him with my finger, and he never withdraws from us unless we have first withdrawn from him. Let us be afraid of such withdrawal. Let us be always with him. Let us live and die with him. Pray to him for me as I do for you.

Yours etc.

November 28, 1690

Fourteenth Letter

To the Same Person

My Dear Mother,

I am distressed to see you suffering so long. What sweetens the compassion I have for your pains, is that I am persuaded that they are proofs of the love God has for you. Regard them in this light, and they will be easy for you. It is my thought that you should abandon all human remedies, and that you surrender yourself completely to divine Providence. God, perhaps, awaits only this surrender, and a perfect confidence in him, to heal you. Since, in spite of all your cares, the remedies have not had the effect they should have had, but, on the contrary, the trouble has grown worse, to put yourself completely in his hands, and to expect all from him, is not 'tempting God'.

I have already said in my last letter that sometimes he allows the body to suffer to heal the malady of our souls. Be courageous. Make a virtue of necessity. Ask God, not to be delivered from the pains of the body, but for the strength to suffer with courage, for his love, all that he shall will, and for as long as it shall please him.

These prayers are, in truth, a little hard on human nature, but most pleasing to God, and sweet to those who love him. Love sweetens sufferings, and when one loves God one suffers for him with joy and courage. Do this, I beg you. Console yourself in him who is the one and only remedy for all our ills. He is the father of the afflicted, always ready to help us. He loves us infinitely more than we think. Love him, then, and seek no other alleviation save in him. I hope you will receive it soon. Farewell. I shall aid you therein by my prayers, poor though they are, and shall always be, in Our Lord,

Yours etc.

P.S. On this Saint Thomas' day I celebrated Holy Communion on your behalf.

Fifteenth Letter

To the Same Person

I thank our Lord for having given you some alleviation, as you have desired. I have been on numerous occasions near to dying, though I have never been so happy. I have, therefore, never asked for relief, but I have asked for the strength to suffer with courage, humility and love. Take courage, my very dear Mother. It is sweet to suffer with God, great though the sufferings be. Take them with love. It is a Paradise to suffer and be with him. Also, if we wish to enjoy, even in this life, the peace of Paradise, we must grow accustomed to a familiar converse, humble and loving, with him. We must prevent our mind wandering away, whatever be the occasion. We must make of our heart a temple of the spirit, where we may worship him continually. We must set unbroken guard over ourselves, that we do nothing, say nothing, think nothing, which could displease him. When we are thus preoccupied with God, sufferings will be only times of happiness, balm and consolation.

I know that, to reach this condition, it is very difficult at the start, that one must act purely in faith. We know, too, that we can do all things with the grace of the Lord, and that he does not refuse it to those who ask him urgently. Knock at the door, keep on knocking, and I say to you that in his own good time, he will open to you, if you are not discouraged, and that he will suddenly give you what he has postponed for many years. Farewell. Pray to him for me, as I do for you. I hope to see him soon. I am, all yours in Our Saviour . . .

January 22, 1691

Sixteenth Letter

To the Same Person

My Good Mother,

God very well knows what is our need, and all he does is for our benefit. If we knew how much he loves us, we should be ever ready to receive equally at his hand the sweet and the bitter. Even the most painful things and the most hard would be sweet and pleasing to us. The direst sufferings appear unbearable to us only from the point of view we hold, and when we are persuaded that it is the hand of God which deals with us, that it is a father full of love who places us in conditions of humiliation, grief and suffering, all the bitterness is removed and they have only sweetness.

Let us give our thoughts completely to knowing God. The more one knows him, the more one wants to know him, and since love is measured commonly by knowledge, then, the deeper and more extensive knowledge shall be, so love will be the greater, and, if love is great, we shall love him equally in suffering and consolation.

Let us not hold ourselves back by seeking or loving God for the favours he bestows upon us, lofty though they can be, or for those he can do for us. These favours, great though they are, will never bring us as near to him as faith does by one simple act. Let us seek him often through this virtue. He is in our midst. Let us seek him nowhere else. Are we not discourteous and guilty of ignoring him, busying ourselves with a thousand thousand trifles which displease, and perhaps which offend him. He endures them all the same, but it is much to be feared that one day they may cost us dearly.

Let us begin by being his without reservation. Let us banish from heart and mind all that which is not himself. He wants to be the only one. Ask of him this grace. If we do, on our part, what we can, we shall soon see the change in us for which we hope. I cannot thank him enough for the small relief he has given you. I hope, by his mercy, for the favour of seeing him in a few days. Let us pray for one another. I am, in Our Lord,

Your etc.

February 6, 1691

PART THREE

The Spiritual Principles of
Brother Lawrence

Translator's Note
The short treatise which forms this third division is
no doubt the writing of Brother Lawrence himself,
perhaps under urgent pressure from his friends. It is
not possible to set out stylistic arguments but these
'maxims' or 'principles' do not read as simply as De
Beaufort's prose. Perhaps with some aid, perhaps
even with a little editing, the small tract sums up, a
trifle repetitively, the recommendations found in the
letters and conversations, and reported by the Abbé
himself. Observe that, here and elsewhere when
Lawrence writes in a third person, he refers to himself.

Spiritual Principles

All things are possible to him who believes, yet more to him who hopes, more still to him who loves, and most of all to him who practises and perseveres in these three virtues. All those who are baptised, and believe as they should, have taken the first step on the road to perfection and will be perfect as long as they continue to observe the following principles:

1. To look always to God and his glory in all that we do, say, and undertake; that the end we seek should be to become faultless worshippers of God in this life as we hope to be throughout eternity; firmly to resolve to overcome with God's grace all the difficulties which confront us in the spiritual life.

2. When we undertake the spiritual life, we must bear in mind who we are, and we shall realise that we are worthy of all scorn, unworthy of the name of Christian, subject to all manner of tribulations, to troublesome circumstances beyond number, which make us uneven in health, moods and disposition of heart and of behaviour, in a word people whom God desires to bring low by countless trials and travail as much within as without.

3. We must without doubt believe that it is to our advantage, that it is pleasing to God to sacrifice us to himself, that it is the way of his divine Providence to allow us to face all manner of situations, to suffer all manner of afflictions and wretchedness, and temptations for the love of God, so long as it shall please him, since, without

this submission of heart and spirit to the will of God, devotion and perfection cannot exist.

4. A soul is the more dependent upon grace according as it aspires to a higher perfection, and God's help is the more necessary at each moment, for without it, it can do nothing; the world, nature and the devil join in a conflict so strong and continuous, that without this present help, and this humble and necessary dependence, they will drag it away in spite of itself; this appears hard to nature but grace accepts it and rests in it.

Practices Essential to Acquire the Spiritual Life

1. The most holy practice, the nearest to daily life, and the most essential for the spiritual life, is the practice of the presence of God, that is to find joy in his divine company and to make it a habit of life, speaking humbly and conversing lovingly with him at all times, every moment, without rule or restriction, above all at times of temptation, distress, dryness, and revulsion, and even of faithlessness and sin.

2. We should apply ourselves continually, so that, without exception, all our actions become small occasions of fellowship with God, yet artlessly, but just as it arises from the purity and the simplicity of the heart.

3. We must do all that we do with thoughtfulness and consideration, without impetuosity or haste,

both of which show an undisciplined spirit; we must work quietly, placidly and lovingly before God, and pray to him to approve our toil, and by this continual attention to God we shall break the Demon's head, and make his weapons fall from his hands.

4. We must, during all our labour and in all else we do, even in our reading and writing, holy though both may be – I say more, even during our formal devotions, and spoken prayers – pause for some short moment, as often indeed as we can, to worship God in the depth of our heart, to savour him, though it be but in passing, and as it were by stealth. Since you are not unaware that God is present before you whatever you are doing, that he is at the depth and centre of your soul, why not then pause from time to time at least from that which occupies you outwardly, even from your spoken prayers, to worship him inwardly, to praise him, petition him, to offer him your heart and thank him? What can God have that gives him greater satisfaction than that a thousand thousand times a day all his creatures should thus pause to withdraw and worship him in the heart. Further, this is to destroy self-love. It can exist only among those things from which these moments of inner withdrawal into God gradually liberate us. Finally we can offer to God no greater witness to our faithfulness than in renouncing and scorning a thousand thousand times the thing created to enjoy a single moment of its Creator. I do not thus seek to compel you to abandon for ever the world about us. Prudence, the mother of virtues, must make the rule; I none the less say that it is a common fault among the

spiritual, not to abandon from time to time the world about us, to savour in peace a few small moments of his divine presence. The digression has been long. I thought the theme needed all this explanation. Let us return to our 'practices'.

5. All these acts of worship must arise from faith, and the belief that in truth God is in our hearts; that we must worship him, love him and serve him in spirit and in truth; that he sees all that which comes to pass, and that will come to pass, in us and in all his creatures; that he exists apart from everything, and is the one on whom all other creatures depend, that he is infinite in all perfection, and merits by his boundless excellence and sovereign power all that which we are, and all that which is in heaven and on earth, all of which he can dispose at his good pleasure in time and eternity. We owe him in justice all our thoughts, words and actions. Let us see that we so act.

6. We must examine with care what are the virtues of which we stand most in need, what are those which are most difficult to win, the sins to which we most often fall, and the most frequent and inevitable occasions of our falling. We must turn to God in complete confidence in the hour of battle, abide strongly in the presence of his divine majesty, worship him humbly, and set before him our woes and our weaknesses. And thus we shall find in him all virtues though we may lack them all.

How We Must Worship God in Spirit and in Truth

This question raises three points which call for an answer: I say:

1. That to worship God in spirit and in truth means to worship God as we should worship him. God is spirit and he must indeed be worshipped in truth – that is to say by a humble and genuine worship of the spirit in the depth and centre of our soul. It is God alone who can see this worship, a worship we can so often repeat that in the end it becomes as it were natural, and as if God were one with our soul and our soul one with God. Practice makes this clear.

2. To worship God in truth is to recognise him for what he is and to recognise ourselves for what we are. To worship God in truth is to recognise in verity and at this moment and in spirit that God is what he is, that is to say infinitely perfect, infinitely to be adored, infinitely removed from evil and thus with every attribute divine. What man shall there be, however small the reason he may have, who will not use all his strength to render to this great God his reverence and his worship?

3. To worship God in truth is again to confess that we are completely separated from him, and that he greatly desires to make us like him if we will. Who will be so unwise as to turn away, even for a moment, from the honour, from the love, the service and the unending worship that we owe to him?

Of the Union of the Soul with God

There are three kinds of union, the first habitual, the second virtual, the third actual.

1. Habitual union is when one is united to God by grace alone.

2. Virtual union is when one begins an action by which one is united to God, and by virtue of that action remains one with him all the time that it continues.

3. Actual union is the most complete, and being entirely spiritual makes its life felt, because the soul is not asleep as in the other modes of union, but feels powerfully active, its motions alive like that of fire, more brilliant than the sun unobscured by cloud. Yet one can be deceived when feeling thus. It is not a mere expression of the heart as if one should say: 'My God, I love you with all my heart' – or other such words. It is an indescribable something of the soul, sweet, peaceful, spiritual, reverent, humble, loving and utterly simple. It lifts the soul and impels it to love God, even to lay hold of him, with emotions beyond description, and which experience alone can make us understand.

4. All those who aim at union with God must know that everything which can refresh the will is welcome and pleasing to it, or contains such. Everyone must admit that God is beyond understanding and that to be one with him the will must be deprived of all manner of tastes and pleasures both spiritual and bodily in order that, being thus stripped, it may be able to love God

above all things. For if the will can in any fashion understand God, it can only be through love. There is a great difference between the tastes and fancies of the will, and the workings of the same will, for the tastes and fancies of the will are in the soul, as though within their own bounds, but its functioning, which is properly love, has its ending in God.

Concerning the Presence of God

1. The presence of God is a directing of our spirit to God or a present remembrance of God which can come about either through the imagination or the understanding.

2. I know a person who for forty years has practised intellectually the presence of God. To this state he gives several other names, calling it sometimes a simple act or a clear and distinct knowledge of God, sometimes a hazy vision of him or a diffuse and loving gaze, a remembering of God. At other times he calls it an alertness towards God, a wordless conversation with him, confidence in God, the life and peace of the soul. Finally this person told me that all these descriptions of the presence of God are no more than synonyms, all meaning the same thing, and that it is now something natural with him. In this way . . .

3. This person says that by dint of actions, and often summoning up his spirit in the presence of God, the habit has so established itself that, as soon as he is free from his common duties and often even when he is deeply engaged in them, the sharp

edge of his spirit, the loftiest part of his soul, without effort on his part, rises above all things, and abides, as though stayed on God, as if in its centre and its place of rest. Feeling almost always his soul in this state of dependence interfused with faith satisfies him, and that is what he calls the actual presence of God. It embraces all the rest and much more, in so much that he now lives as if there were only God and he in the world. He converses everywhere with God, asks only for what he has need and is refreshed endlessly in a thousand thousand ways.

4. Now is is right to know that this fellowship with God takes place in the depth and centre of the soul. It is there that the soul speaks to God heart to heart, and always amid a great deep peace in which the spirit revels in God. Everything which happens without is to the soul no more than a fire of straw which is burned out as fast as it blazes, and hardly ever, or very little, disturbs the peace within.

5. To return to our theme of the presence of God, I say that this gentle loving gaze of God, insensibly lights a fire divine in the soul, which so warmly kindles it with the love of God that one is constrained to temper it with many outward acts.

6. We should be quite astonished if we knew what the soul sometimes says to God, who seems so to delight in such conversations, that he permits all, provided the soul abides always with him, and in his inner being, and, as if he feared lest the soul should return to earthly things, he takes care to provide for it everything it can desire, so well that it often finds within itself a meat most savoury and delicious to its taste, though it has not desired

nor sought it in any way, and without, on its part, contributing anything but simple willingness to receive.

7. The presence of God is then, the life and nourishment of the soul, which may win it by the Lord's grace – as follows:

Means of Attaining the Presence of God

1. The first means is a great purity of life.
2. The second is a great faithfulness in the practice of this presence, and in keeping the soul's gaze on God, within which always all is done quietly, humbly, lovingly, and without giving way to any disturbance or anxiety.
3. In the matter of this inner gaze, special care must be taken that it comes before, be it but momentarily, your outer actions, that at times it goes with them, and that you end them all in like manner. Since it takes time and much toil to acquire this practice, so one must not be disturbed when one fails, for the habit does not form save with trouble, so when it is established it can give great joy. Is it not right that the heart, which comes first to life, which is lord over the rest of the body's members, should be both the first and the last to love and worship God, both in beginning and ending what we do in the spirit and the flesh, and generally throughout all the processes of life? And it is here that we must take care to ensure this small looking within, an exercise, as I have said, not without the toil and trouble which facilitates it.

4. It will not be inappropriate for those who undertake this practice, to resort in the heart to a few words such as: 'My God, I am wholly yours'; 'God of love, I love you with all my heart'; 'Lord, fashion me according to your heart' – or such other words as love may suggest at the moment. But they must take care lest their mind wander and return to the world around. They must keep it fastened on God alone, so that, seeing itself thus constrained and controlled by the will, in the end it finds itself constrained to abide in God.

5. This practice of God's presence, somewhat difficult at the start, if maintained faithfully, produces secretly in the soul wonderful effects, draws thither in abundance the graces of the Lord, and leads it imperceptibly to that simple grace, that loving vision of an ever-present God, which is the holiest, most real, easy and effective way to pray.

6. Observe, please, that to attain this condition, the control of the senses is taken for granted, since it is impossible that the soul which retains some affection for earthly things, should enjoy to the full this divine presence, for to be with God it is needful to abandon absolutely that which is created.

The Benefits of the Presence of God

1. The first benefit that the soul receives from the presence of God, is that faith becomes more alive and active in all the processes of our life, particularly in our needs, since it wins for us grace in our temptations, and in the inevitable relationships with our fellows, for the soul, accustomed by this

exercise to the practice of faith, by a simple act of memory, sees and feels that God is there, calls on him easily and meaningfully, and obtains that which it needs. It might be said that herein it approaches something of the state of the Blessed, and the more it goes forward the more its faith becomes alive, and at last becomes so penetrating that one might almost say: 'I no longer believe, I see and I experience.'

2. The practice of the presence of God makes us stronger in hope. Our hope grows in proportion to our knowledge, and according as our faith penetrates, through this holy exercise into the secrets of the Divine, so it discovers in God a beauty which not only infinitely surpasses any visible earthly body, but also that of the most perfect souls and that of the angels. Our hope grows and strengthens itself and the grandeur of this good which it seeks to enjoy, and in some manner tastes, reassures and sustains it.

3. Hope imbues the will with a scorn for earthly things, and kindles it with the fire of sacred love, because, being always with God who is a consuming fire, it burns to ashes whatever stands against it. This soul, thus kindled, can only go on living in the presence of its God, a presence which engenders in its heart a holy ardour, a sacred eagerness and longing to see this God loved, known, served and worshipped by all creatures.

4. By the practice of God's presence and this inner gaze the soul becomes familiar with God in such fashion that it passes almost all its life in continual acts of love, worship, contrition, trust, acts of thankfulness, sacrifice, petition and all the noblest virtues. Sometimes the soul becomes a

single unceasing act, because it is always in the unbroken exercise of this divine presence.

5. I know that few are found who reach this level. It is a grace which God bestows only on a few chosen souls, for in the end that 'simple gaze' is a gift of his liberal hand. But I shall say for the consolation of those who wish to embrace this holy practice, that he commonly gives it to those who set themselves to receive it, and if he does not give it, one can at least, with the help of his common grace, acquire, by the practice of the presence of God, a fashion and state of prayer, very close to that 'simple gaze'.

PART FOUR

The Ways of Brother Lawrence

Translator's Note
This translation, as the two parentheses at the end indicate, omits a few pages in which the narrator becomes too prominent for the effectiveness of the real story. The Abbé writes better than he does in the initial Eulogy, which has been completely passed by, for the reasons indicated. It is smooth enough French. Those were, after all, the years in which that powerful and subtle language reached a peak of elegant simplicity.

The Ways of Brother Lawrence

I write of what I have heard and seen personally of the ways of Brother Lawrence, Barefoot Carmelite, who died in the Convent of Paris about two years ago and whose memory is a blessing.

A person who preferred to end his life in the least place of the house of God, than to hold high rank among sinners, who chose rather the reproach of Jesus Christ than the vain show and pleasures of Egypt, has expressed the wish that I share with souls undeceived by the love of this present age, that which he knew I had collected of the thoughts of Brother Lawrence. I acquiesce gladly. And although I have already published a Eulogy and some Letters of this good Brother, I have concluded that what we have preserved of this holy man, cannot be too widely expanded.

I have thought it would be helpful to reveal in his person an excellent model of sturdy piety, in a time when almost everyone locates virtue where it is not, and takes false paths by which to reach it. It will be Brother Lawrence who shall speak to you himself. I shall give you his very words in the conversations I have had with him. I wrote them down as soon as I had left him. No one depicts the saints better than they do themselves. The Confessions and the Letters of Saint Augustine makes a portrait of him much more natural than anything else which could be said about him, so nothing will make better known the servant of God, whose virtues I wish to describe to you, than what he himself said in his heart's simplicity.

The worth of Brother Lawrence did not make him at all stern. He had a friendly welcome which gave confidence, and the immediate feeling that one could confide everything to him, and that one had found a friend. On his part, when he knew those with whom he had to do, he spoke with freedom and showed great kindness. What he said was simple, but always to the point and full of sense. Beneath a rough exterior could be perceived a freedom beyond the ordinary reach of a poor Lay Brother, an insight which surpassed all that one expected of him. In seeking charity, he showed an intelligence fit to conduct the most important business, and which was available for all manner of consultation. Such was Brother Lawrence on first acquaintance.

He has himself revealed his character, and his inner ways in the conversations I have presented to you. His conversion began as you will find noted there, by a lofty idea he conceived of the power and wisdom of God. This he cultivated carefully with a great faithfulness which dismissed every other thought.

Since this first knowledge of God was, in the outcome, the basic principle of all Brother Lawrence's perfection, it is relevant to pause a little at that point to consider his conduct in relation to it. Faith was the only light he used, not only to know God in the beginning – he wished never to do other than employ faith to teach and guide himself in all the ways of God. He told me often that everything he heard others say, and everything he found in books, all that he wrote himself, seemed insipid compared with the grandeur of God and Jesus Christ, which faith would reveal to him. To quote him: 'He alone is able to make himself known as he really is. We seek in reasoning and in the sciences, as in a bad copy, for what we neglect to see in an excellent original. God depicts himself in the depths of our soul, and we are not willing to see him there. We leave him for trifles, and disdain to hold converse with our King, who is always present in us. It is too little to love God and to know him by what books tell us, or by what we feel within, through a few worshipful ideas, or some inspiration. We must bring our faith to life, and by means of it lift ourselves above all that which we feel, to worship God and Jesus Christ in all their divine perfections, as they are in themselves. This path of faith is the spirit of the Church, and is sufficient for us to reach high perfection.'

Not only would he look on God as present in his soul by faith, but in all that he saw, in all that happened to him, he raised his heart at once, passing from the thing created to its Creator. A tree that he saw leafless in winter made him think immediately of God, and planted in him a notion so sublime, that, when he recalled it to me after forty years, it was an idea still as strong and vivid in his soul as when he first conceived it. Such was his way on all occasions, using visible things to reach the invisible.

Thus, too in the the little reading which he did, he preferred the Holy Gospel to all other books, for there, in the very words of Jesus Christ, he found most simply and most purely that with which to nourish his faith. It was by faithfulness in cultivating in his heart the deep presence of God, considered by faith, that Brother Lawrence began. He occupied himself with continued acts of worship and of love, and in calling for help from Our Lord, in all he had to do. He would thank him when he had done it, and asked pardon for his shortcomings by confessing them, without 'making excuses to God'. Since all this was so bound to what he did, and what he did provided the material, he did his work with greater ease. Far from distracting him from his work, the practice enabled him to do well. He confessed, however, that it was hard at the outset. and that there were considerable times when he would forget his exercise. After confessing humbly his fault, he took it up again without trouble.

Sometimes a host of undisciplined thoughts would violently take over the place of God, and he was satisfied to set them gently aside to return to his customary communion. Finally his faithfulness won the reward of an unbroken remembrance of God. His many and varied doings were changed into a simple vision, an enlightened love, an unbroken enjoyment. As he would say: 'The time of action does not differ from that of prayer. I possess God as peacefully in the bustle of my kitchen, where sometimes several people are asking me for different things at the same time, as I do upon my knees before the Holy Sacrament. My faith even becomes so enlightened that I think I have lost it. It seems to me that the curtain of obscurity is drawn, and that the endless cloudless day of the other life is dawning.' This is the point to which his faithfulness in rejecting every other thought, in order to devote himself to continual converse with God, had led our good Brother. At last it had become so habitual with him, that it was almost impossible, he would say, to turn away from it and attend to other matters.

In these conversations you will find an important observation on this matter. This practice of the presence of God, he said, 'must stem from the heart, from love rather than from the understanding and speech. In the way of God, thought counts for little. Love does everything and it is not needful to have great things to do.' (These are the words, if you will permit me to quote him directly, of a Lay Brother in the kitchen.) 'I turn my little omelette in the pan for the love of God. When it is finished, if I have nothing to do, I prostrate myself on the ground and worship my God, who gave me the grace to make it, after which I arise happier than a king. When I can do nothing else, it is enough to have picked up a straw for the love of God. People look for ways of learning how to love God. They hope to attain it by I know not how many different practices. They take much trouble to abide in his presence by varied means. Is it not a shorter and more direct way to do everything for the love of God, to make use of all the tasks one's lot in life demands to show him that love, and to maintain his presence within by the communion of our heart with his? There is nothing complicated about it. One has only to turn to it honestly and simply.' (Reverently I retain his own words.)

We must not, however, suppose that to love God it is enough to offer him his works, to invoke his aid and produce acts of love for him. Our Brother reached love's perfection only because he had been careful, right from the beginning, to do nothing which could displease God, and because he had renounced all else and had entirely forgotten himself. 'Since my entrance into religion' (to use his own words again) 'I have ceased to think of virtue or of my own salvation. After having given myself wholly to God in satisfaction for my sins, and for the love of him renounced all that is apart from him, I have believed that for the rest of my life I had one duty only – to live as if there was no one but me and God in the world.'

Thus Brother Lawrence began in the most perfect way, abandoning all for God, and doing all for the love of him. He forgot himself totally, and thought no longer of Heaven or Hell, nor of his past sins, nor of those he would commit after he had asked God's pardon for them. He never went back over his confessions. He entered into perfect peace when he had confessed his sins to God. He knew of nothing else to do. After that he left himself in God's hands for life, death, time and eternity. 'We are made for God alone. God would not think it wrong for us to abandon ourselves and devote ourselves entirely to him. In him we shall see better what we lack than we could perceive in ourselves by all our meditations. It can only be in us a remnant of self-love which, under the guise of our perfection, binds us still to self, and hinders us from lifting our hearts to God.'

The Brother used to say that, in the great anguish he had suffered for four years so great that no one alive could have freed his mind from the conviction that he would be lost, he had not changed at all his first resolution, but that, without thinking of what would become of him, and without thought of his anguish (as all souls in anguish do), he had consoled himself by saying: 'Whatever happens, I will do everything I do, for the rest of my life, out of love for God.' Thus forgetting himself, he had been ready to be lost for God, in whom he had truly found himself.

The love of God's will in him, had taken the place of the attachment one commonly has for one's own will. In all that happened to him he would see the plan of God, and this kept him in unbroken peace. When someone would tell him of some great disorder, instead of being amazed at it, he was on the contrary surprised that it was not worse, in view of the evil of which the sinner is capable. At once lifting his heart to God, and seeing that he could remedy the situation, and yet allowed these evils to take place, for the most just and salutary reasons in the general ordering of his control of the world, after praying for the sinner concerned, he distressed himself no more about it and remained at peace.

One day I told him, without preparation, that something of great consequence which he had very close to his heart, and for which he had worked for a long time, could not be done, and that a resolution against the proposal had been adopted. To this he simply replied: 'It must be accepted that those who thus decided have good reasons. It only remains to carry it out, and say no more about it.' This in fact he did, and so completely that, although he has since had frequent occasions to mention it, he has never said a word.

A man of very high standing, visiting Brother Lawrence during a serious illness, asked him what he would choose if God made him the offer either to leave him for a time longer alive in order to increase his merits, or to be received forthwith in heaven. Without considering, the good Brother replied that he would leave that choice to God and that for him he had nothing else to do but to wait in peace until God should show his will.

This attitude of mind left him in such great indifference to everything and in liberty so complete that it approached that of the Blessed Ones. He belonged to no party. No bent or preference was to be found in him. The natural attachment to his country, which people carry with them even into the most holy offices, did not concern him. He was equally loved by those who had the opposite inclinations. He wished for good in general without regard for persons, by whom, or for whom it was done. As a Citizen of Heaven, nothing bound him on earth. His outlook was not limited by time. After long contemplation of no one but the Eternal One, he had become eternal like him.

Everything was the same to him, every place, every task. The good Brother found God everywhere, as much while he was repairing shoes as while he was praying with the Community. He was not eager to go into retreat, for he found in his common tasks the same God to worship as in the depths of the deserts. His whole means of approach to God was to do all for the love of him, and so he was not concerned about that which claimed his attention, provided that he did it for God. It was God, not the task, he had in view. He knew that, the more the task was against his natural inclinations, the greater was his love in offering it to God, and that the smallness of the deed would in no way diminish the value of his offering, because God, having need of nothing, would only consider in what he did the love which went with it.

Another feature of Brother Lawrence's character was an extraordinary firmness, which in another walk of life would have been termed fearlessness. It revealed a great soul, lifted above the fear and the hope of all that which was not God. He wondered at nothing; nothing astonished him; he feared nothing. This steadfastness of soul flowed from the same source as all his other virtues. The exalted notion which he had of God set God forth to him as indeed God is – sovereign justice and infinite goodness. Supported by these he was assured that God would not deceive him, and would only bring him good, since he, for his part was resolved not to displease him ever, but to do all and endure all for the love of him.

I asked of him one day who was his Director. He replied that indeed he had none, and thought he had no need of one, since the rule and the duties he had as a monk indicated what he had to do in common life, and the Gospel required him to love God with all his heart. As he knew this, a Director seemed to have no purpose for him – but he had great need of a Confessor for the remission of his sins.

Those who conduct themselves in the spiritual life according to their inclinations or personal sentiments, and think they have nothing more important to do than examine themselves to see whether they are properly devout or not, such folk will never know stability, nor a fixed rule of life, because such things change continually, either through our own negligence, or because God so orders it. He varies his gifts and his manner of dealing with us according to our needs.

The good Brother, on the contrary, firm on the path of faith, which never changes, was always the same, because he sought only to fulfil his duties in the place where God put him, counting as merit only the virtues which that condition required. Instead of taking notice of his inclinations and examining the path beneath his feet, he looked only to God, the goal of this path, and strode towards him by the practice of justice, charity and humility, busier in doing than thinking of what he was doing.

The devotion of Brother Lawrence, based on this firm foundation, was not dependent on visions, or other extraordinary experiences. He was persuaded that even those which were genuine, are often the signs of a soul's weakness, which pauses rather at the gift of God than before God himself. Apart from the period of his novitiate, none of these experiences entered his life – at least he mentioned none to those in whom he had most trust, and to whom he opened his heart. All through life he trod in the footsteps of the saints on the sure path of faith. It was not that he departed from the common way of salvation by the exercises from all time sanctioned by the Church, by the practice of good works, and the virtues proper to his condition, but all else he distrusted. His great common sense, and the light he drew from the simplicity of his faith, protected him from all the reefs which are found in the course of the spirit, on which so many souls are wrecked today, because they give themselves to love of novelty, curiosity, and the guidance of men.

(At this point some three hundred and fifty words of Monsieur l'Abbé Joseph de Beaufort are omitted. They stray from the theme. Honestly trying to allow Brother Lawrence to speak, the good man has been unable to suppress a fear that too wide and undisciplined an acceptance of Brother Lawrence's ways might diminish the authority and the prestige of the Church. He has 'weaker brethren' in mind, and permits himself a disquisition on potential deviance, on the rôle of the Church, and the nature of its tolerance. Perhaps the Archbishop so directed. Perhaps the Abbé shared an uneasiness, and no doubt such a hint was not unwelcome to a good churchman somewhat given to wordiness. To resume:)

Prepared by such a life, and following so sure a course, he saw the coming of death without distress.

His patience had been very great all through his life, but it grew when he drew near to the end. He seemed never to have a moment of sorrow, even in the greatest violence of his malady Joy was evident not only on his face, but also in his manner of speaking, so much so that members of the Community who went to visit him were constrained to ask whether actually he was not in pain. 'Pardon', he said, 'I *am* in pain. The place in my side hurts. But my soul is content.' But they went on: 'If God wanted you to endure these pains for the space of ten years would you be content?' 'I would bear it', he replied, 'not only for that number of years. If God willed that I endure my woes until Judgment day, I would willingly consent, and would still hope that he would give me grace always to be content.'

With the hour for his departure from this world approaching, he cried again and again: 'Faith, faith', expressing thus its excellence better than if he had said more. He worshipped God ceaselessly, and said to a brother that it was hardly any longer a *belief* that God dwelt in his soul. By the light of faith he already saw something of this intimate presence. His fearlessness was so great during a voyage in which there is everything to fear, that he said to a friend who questioned him on this matter, that he feared neither death, Hell nor the judgment of God, nor the efforts of the Devil. As they liked to hear him say such helpful words, they went on with their questions. One asked him whether he knew that it was a fearful thing to fall into the hands of the living God, because no one at all is sure whether he is worthy of love or hatred. 'Agreed', he said, 'but I would not want to know, for fear of vanity. Nothing is better than to abandon oneself to God.'

After he had received the Last Sacraments a brother asked him what he was doing, and what occupied his spirit. 'I am doing', he replied, 'what I shall do through all eternity. I am blessing God, praising him, worshipping him, and loving him with all my heart. That is all our profession, brothers, to worship God, to love him, without troubling ourselves with anything else.'

Such were the last words of Brother Lawrence, who died a little afterwards with the peace and tranquillity with which he had lived. His death took place on February 11, 1691, when he was about eighty years old.

(Monsieur l'Abbé lacked an eye for a good ending. He has told his story, not without some unnecessary intrusions, and should have left it there to speak powerfully, for itself. He was unable to deny himself a discourse on the great Christian sages, and to express a pious wonder that a man so humble should, in the wisdom of God, have found a place in their exalted company. Not without some display of patristic erudition, he quotes his august heroes, and points out their virtues. He underlines those traits and features which Christians generally who have read about the gentle monastery cook might find it possible, indeed obligatory, to weave into the pattern of their own lives. If they have read the story, they have already sensed that appeal and challenge. Instead of reading some twelve hundred words of Joseph de Beaufort's musing, most readers would prefer to leave it there, close the little book and think. Even Sister Mary David cannot bring herself to translate more than half, and, of the translators into English I have been able to unearth, she is the most tolerant with the wordy narrator. She includes even the Eulogy. So it is farewell, Brother Lawrence. You have spoken well. It was nine o'clock in the morning and the trumpets must have sounded on the other side.)